TIGERS
and the
CEO

ESSENTIAL POETS SERIES 220

**Canada Council
for the Arts**

**Conseil des Arts
du Canada**

Guernica Editions Inc. acknowledges the
support of the Canada Council for the Arts
and the Ontario Arts Council. The Ontario
Arts Council is an agency of the Government
of Ontario.

We acknowledge the financial support of the
Government of Canada through the Canada
Book Fund (CBF) for our
publishing activities.

**ONTARIO ARTS COUNCIL
CONSEIL DES ARTS DE L'ONTARIO**

an Ontario government agency
un organisme du gouvernement de l'Ontario

Cristina Perissinotto

TIGERS
and the
CEO

GUERNICA

TORONTO – BUFFALO – LANCASTER (U.K.)
2014

Michael Mirolla, editor
Guernica Editions Inc.
P.O. Box 76080, Abbey Market, Oakville, (ON), Canada L6M 3H5
2250 Military Road, Tonawanda, N.Y. 14150-6000 U.S.A.

Distributors:
University of Toronto Press Distribution,
5201 Dufferin Street, Toronto (ON), Canada M3H 5T8
Gazelle Book Services, White Cross Mills, High Town, Lancaster LA1 4XS
U.K.

First edition.
Printed in Canada.

Legal Deposit – Third Quarter
Library of Congress Catalog Card Number: 2014934794
Library and Archives Canada Cataloguing in Publication
Perissinotto, Cristina, author
Tigers and the CEO / Cristina Perissinotto.

(Essential poets series ; 220)
Poems.
Issued in print and electronic formats.
ISBN 978-1-55071-921-5 (pbk.).--ISBN 978-1-55071-922-2 (epub).--
ISBN 978-1-55071-923-9 (mobi)

I. Title. II. Series: Essential poets series ; 220

PS8631.E7337T55 2014   C811'.6   C2014-900238-6
                                                C2014-900239-4

To those who dream utopian dreams,
this book is for you.

Contents

Acknowledgements

This collection was born of two main events: the first one was my discovery, within the literary tradition of Indian magical realism, of its metaphorical usage of tigers. The second one was my chance encounter with a tiger-hunting CEO.

I am grateful to the House of Literature (Σπίτι της Λογοτεχνίας) in Paros, Greece and the Writers' Center in Rhodes, Greece, for their support, hospitality, and the touching beauty of the landscape.

I am grateful for the Canadian winters, when most of these poems were first conceived, for the concentration they provided. I also wish to acknowledge the journals that have kindly given space to my work, in particular *Miranda* for publishing "Ecotourism."

My gratitude to Montreal's Poetry Plus for appreciating my work and encouraging me, and to my parents, who will never read this book unless I translate it into Italian, but think it's a masterpiece anyway.

Travelling Love

The little hands of your phone,
smaller than the rain, reach inside
of me from Morristown, the very moment
I twist open a bottle of Fiuggi.
You are so much closer, just on the other side
of the border.

You call me at funny hours, tell me you like me so,
make plans to see me in Venice next month,
do I prefer the Lido or Rialto
or would I like to see you in Milan instead?

You'll drive any distance, you'll come and see me
in person, in my flesh and pink cheeks.

Travelling love. While you work your magic
in Arizona, here in Ottawa the snow comes down
in large, wet flakes. I pick up the phone
and honour the destiny of a love that travels.
Of solitude and readings, of mineral water
and emails, of phone calls and faith.

In Dublin

Winds blow from the East
above the river Liffey (ne'er too pretty
when the tide is out) and ruffle
the drip-dry clothes of the American tourists
and the red locks resting on the breasts
of Celtic maidens.

At times I take refuge in the Am Bia café
which enwraps me in a cozy, dill-infused embrace.

I can read here, books of poetry and hope
strife and life; as they prepare their salmon soup
the waiters speak Gaelic
useful for recipes and spell casting.

What is the name of this wind that brings
tears to my eyes, weakness to my knees?
Have I been here before, and how do they say
love in Gaelic?

Joy

Sometimes I wander into the wolfmother room
of my wolftale – the one I've just
barely sketched with office markers and night calls.

Our budding love feels like my home in Ottawa
brimming with possibilities, temporarily bare.

You are getting the biggest share of my imagination
you call me joy, over the phone.

Milan

With my finger I trace
the silhouette of his body,
the birthmak on his lower back
his sturdy calves; I listen
to his soft snoring.

He sees me come and go
weep and mourn
our temporary separations.
He pats me on the shoulder
come on come on,
we'll see each other again
soon as we can.

Every 20 minutes
a streetcar rumbles outside the window.
He turns around in the bed,
opens his eyes for a second,
mumbles what time is it.
It's 3:25, I answer.
He smiles, and goes back to sleep.

Autumn Still

Not much gets accomplished this early.
I make tea, while Saturday
is dark and deliberate
like a mourning widow.

On my desk, calendar pages sing
their nostalgia for lost days,
the books call me babe, the computer
grunts and speaks to me in tongues.

My inner child is kvetching
dead tired of my lies.
The weather accomplishes
some snow.

Blame the Sheep

"Thomas More blamed the sheep
for England's lack of communal spaces,
for neglecting to feed its poor
for ignoring the ancient rights of the people."
This I told Biral, my advisor, his eyes a shade of blue
so deep it was almost black.
"He complained that sheep were eating men."
I pressed on, the eagerness of a young cub
having caught its first fish: "He had socialist ideas."

His sharp profile was only partly
softened by Venice's afternoon sun,
"Oh," he answered, "what do you know,
socialist ideals in the English Renaissance."
A hint of a smile at the corner of his mouth.
"I'll bet," he mused, "that nobody
had voiced such a deep concern before,
for the poor getting poorer,
and the rich, richer."

Sulphur

The sulphur factory
of which he was king
was shrouded in fog.

An industrial Avalon, brightened
by his presence. Smokestacks released
white vapour plumes towards
the blustery sky.

A large pipe poured warm water
into the nearby creek.
There's fish in this river, he said
we'll go fishing one of these days.

Sulphur, steam, icy clouds
and his luminous smile.

His Voice

His voice uncoils ensnarls enraptures
me, as I curl up on the couch.
He's the ancestral snake, his words
a dance. Hypnotic, ravishing,
a sangha – hypnotic,
distended, buried deep
somewhere in my mind.

Years Later

Years later people will find
them in many places – letters, notes,
silver rings, pebbles, shreds of postcards.
Because of the obsessive-compulsive
literacy of the writer(s), nothing
of importance was ever thrown away.
Because of the scatter-mindedness
of all those involved, nothing
was catalogued, but strewn
every which way, in different cities,
spanning two continents and a few
web servers.

Few precious photographs, evidence
that something had taken place
and that the lymph of life had rushed
through their veins like tropical rain.

But the collector, the curious souls,
the niece or nephew with an inclination
for family history – she might have a chance
to collect and catalogue papers, correspondence
and early, unicoded emails
whereupon she might find enough evidence
of the intensity of love and the sadness of betrayal.

The bodies of those involved will rest
someplace where it no longer matters.
Their souls, with a little luck
will be incarnated in superior beings

in reunited bodies, able of revelling
in the beauty of each other, of making a good go
at life together; they will learn how to atone
for the sorrows of previous attempts,
and make it work, make it work, the next time around.

Fall in Venice

In the fall the canal shimmered
under the Ponte dei Miracoli,
fish turned golden and ate
from people's hands.

Scorpions on the windowsill
sang a lonely tune
and you and I kissed at every arch
in the Rio delle Maravegie.

In the golden light of the early spring
I failed to see that you would leave anyway
that miracles never happened in October.

For the Love of Languages

The department had already migrated,
from the old convent of San Sebastiano
to a Baroque palace by the Gran Canal.
Coming home, I was a preening duckling,
giddy from stealing a glimpse
of his blue eyes, a speck of his dark soul.
My advisor, torn asunder by his own genius.

Walking back, on a hunch I called home.
He's here, my roommate whispered,
should I tell him to wait.

So I told her: give me a few minutes, I'll be right
there. And I ran, past the Accademia bridge
and through Campo San Polo, breathless
up the little bridge leading to my apartment.
There he was, dangling his left shoe.

He had a smile. That bearded shiny smile
that dazzled the world. Gave me a note
he had written while waiting.
"I wanted to surprise you, today.
As it turned out, I only surprised myself.
I'll hang out with the gals in the kitchen
for a while, hoping you'll be back, soon."
"Gals," I had to look up in the dictionary.

Today I called him and he was
not home. I told his machine that I wanted
to surprise him, and as it turned out, I just
surprised myself. Those words, uttered for me
years ago, came out as if congenitally
ingrained. We learn languages, I believe,
in discrete segments. They cluster around
precise moments, expression crystallize
around loved ones.

Do you know who taught you
how to say "love"? Of course not
you were too little. But try to master
another language.

Each new expression is recalled
together with the face of its teacher.
I know who taught me how to say "more"
with the proper inflection – that was also
the bearded one, one rainy afternoon
we spent at home.

In Praise of Italian Kids

Kids around here are beautiful.
Like all God's children, sometimes
they need shoes.
So I take my neighbours' kid, Simone,
to the local pharmacy-shoe store,
where a *signorina*
fits him with blue sandals.

My mom wrinkles her nose, not elegant enough,
she says, while Simone cooperates congenially
by helping the *signorina* in her fitting job.

When we finally pick a pair
he is bored and thirsty,
so we walk down the street to Cancian Bar.
Simone gets a glass of Coca-Cola
with a slice of lemon.
My mom and I have ice coffee in a chalice.
This is the life. All around,
Vespas and noisy trucks;
we enjoy the view and the exhaust fumes.

I tell my mom, how are we going to live
in this world without kids of our own.
It's genetic death. Perhaps,
your brother and Julia
will take care of it, she replies.
Simone is blowing bubbles with his straw.
Take care of what, he asks.

In the Land of Marco Polo

Early summer. Lush with improbable
designer trees, the countryside resists
the urban sprawl.
The land gives out that nightly smell
breathes dripping breaths
as ducklings paddle slowly through river weeds.

They say many a thing about this town,
none of which is true.
They say it was named after the cranes
that were plentiful in the river
until Attila and his Huns swooped down
and roasted them all on a spit.

They say it is the Bronx of Northern Italy
drugs and prostitution tucked away in every corner.
But it is not true. I have visited the Bronx once
and some parts were quiet and suburban
and shrouded in a white blanket. Just like here,
minus the snow.

I visit the abbeys in the area,
walk ancient walks and take note of Roman ruins.
Knowledge is no panacea for loneliness,
although port of cranes – Portogruaro –
is showing a charm it never had.

Some days the sky turns so menacingly dark
that my papers sprout wings and fly all over the room.
When I was a child, growing up here, I longed
to get away. To write articles on airplanes,
know the name of each big city's main street:
Magnificent Mile, Paseo De Gracia, Ste-Catherine.
But I had not read *Invisible Cities* yet, that obscure
passage where Kublai Khan asks Marco Polo,
what has all your travelling been good for?

How the Opaque Lover

How the opaque lover
became a hologram of distance, this
I'll never know.

White was the restaurant on the river
warm were his hands, loving his eyes
healing the bread we broke at the table
drunk were we, thirsty for each other's
words like puppy seals for mama's milk.

Soon his attention turned mutable
like April rains, now with me
now gone.

An alchemy of distance. Only seldom
did he miss my voice; a blue couch
cradled the time spent
whispering to him on the phone.
My bed framed his absence.

His text messages popped up
inside my phone like crackerjacks.
Once in a while I stepped out of my skin
and travelled to Venice, just to forget him.
At times I almost did.

Impenetrable lover. My window framed
the Rideau river besieged by ice.

Mostly, he disappeared as I alighted,
he sought out my voice when I travelled far,
never again, never again in my arms.

Once I asked for his boyhood picture
he sent several – boy at the beach building
sandcastles, boy with mom in perfect,
1960s hairdo, boy holding a lion cub.

How could the upper-class boy
not love me back, I wondered as
the streets on campus whitened
and the seagulls in Strathcona Park
walked me home.

By day I hoped that he'd think
of me, if only fleetingly;
in class, at home, in little cafés
filled with people oblivious
of his wondrous existence.

Little did he know about my
perpetual border crossing, about
the eternal sunrise over the Alps
as my plane approached Europe.

Some instinct alerted him
when I drew closer,
yet he was skillful in the alchemy
of happiness – crackerjacks going off
in my cell phone, my heart beating
faster, his fingers typing rapidly –
"ciao gioia, sei in Italia?"

Love Me

Hazy mornings. Not-quite-July, though the heat
blazes its way from the tropics, and life is
a whisper of milk in a teacup.

Love me. Milan swallows you in a life so obscure
my imagination falters. Outside my window
not-yet-July bubbles fiercely.

I struggle with this hunger. Green leaves
pierced heart, humidity like a night in Pernambuco.
Please love me, I would say breezily
if I could only talk to you
one more time.

Tigers and the CEO

So busy with his own wheeling and dealing
doing especially well with money
by day, with women by night.

Some men might need more feelings,
more soul than this endless prowling,
this tiger-munching, this intense business
of being loved without loving back.

But he's king, hakuna matata, crunching deals
by day, munching by night.
And it's, by the way, never again with you, *gioia*,
your life is too wanting, your hunger
too tangible, sacred, lyrical, terrifying.
I'm sorry *gioia*, you're nice, but never again.

The naked soul could roam its longest nights
craving his voice, yearning for his lower tones,
for the rough fabric of his inflection.
Roaming, wandering, she prowls
the night replaying his ideas on high finance,
on the business of doing business.
The CEO in a flawless suit
delivering most competent speeches,
charm and testosterone, tigernip.

Her soul meanders to the portal of a baroque church
asking to please please let her in. But never
again *gioia*, the CEO is too busy with money,
with his villas, with all the women
who take to his growling like a bulimic takes to pie.

The CEO is a man of taste,
the one to welcome the blue-eyed governor
when he comes to town.

Expensive tapestry in his office
in ethnic, sub-saharan colors.
Reddish marks streak the heart of her days
she's haunted by tigers she doesn't know.
His soul will miss her, she assures herself,
yet her psyche wanders about
knocking at his temple's portal.

Remotely regal, luscious and absent
aloof like a Chow-Chow, fierce and sentimental
in the preliminary phases, cold and poised in the closing.
The CEO and his sweet words, certainties
so sturdy no life storm will ever bend.

Every phase of his inaccessible life is tabooed
with interdictions, numbers crop up like rational magic.
He's the sudoku grand master; his quabbalah always
turns into more gain. Other souls, other tigers
waft in and out of his smart phone. Pouty lips,
breasts and bellies that sometimes
carry babies to be born. But you're out
of his contact list *gioia*, it's never again with you.

When was it that he unlearned to speak with her,
that he forgot her phone number, when did her existence
slip out of his mind. One day, he might remember.
He might chance upon some old emails, he might close
the deal of his life.
Perhaps he'll realize that the buds of his tree
are getting close to full bloom, and that there is pruning
and grafting to do.

He may decide to graft her onto his life, long
sinuous leaves shining and unfolding like a Spanish fan.
A sudden ring will wake her one morning
and she'll hear the soft uncoiling of his voice
his words pouring in like the first glass of water.
Perhaps a catch in her voice will disclose
how much international finance makes her weep.

Right now, she looks at maps of remote
constellations, trying to make sense of the cipher
of their distance. She traces them with her finger
when she walks at night, gets to know them this way.

Trading Places

I would trade places with you
just to see you once in passing
you migrating towards this frigid peninsula
to the snow that you so love.

Just to see your boots
anticipate the crunch of the earth,
the glory of its whiteness
the soft shattering of ice formations
at each step.

Just to watch you visit the library
on Saturdays, busy fingers
type-A nervousness
your life awaiting
outside with baited breath.

Just to see you arrive at Dorval
with suitcases and Chocolate Labrador
and laptop and impatience,
and your little family
of which I am no part.

Just to get a glimpse
of you in the landed crowd.
As if trading places were possible,
and our life a complicated game of GO.

Highway 45

Leaving Nashville where – they say –
all radio stations play the same tune.
Hills with white-porched houses
tucked in their cleavages.
This could easily be Umbria on a rainy day,
give or take a cow
or a donkey, drudging over yonder.
But the stereo whispers Feelin' Groovy,
not Santa Lucia.

Highway 45 unwinds like an oversize eel.
Four to six lanes wide,
it raises and lowers ever so slightly.
Smooth like melted chocolate, Amy ponders,
reaching for the M&M's on the dashboard.
Cathy, from the CD, smiles approvingly
at the metaphor.

Like a steel blade the road
cuts through the land between the lakes,
shaving hilltops that throb with stunning reds,
kiss you on the forehead with feverish yellows.
Cecilia, while breaking someone's heart
from the loudspeakers, kicks back
and enjoys the view.

When we reach the bridges on the Ohio
it's my father that speaks through me
in awe. Two perfect domes caress
the clouds' gray underbelly.
The sound of silence merges
with the river rushing through.
Everyone should live by a river,
I tell Amy. Or by a mountain, she says,
while the sun sets over the closest range.

The Leaves and the Manuscript

Somewhere in the deep gorges of Delphi
there's a sheath of laurel leaves,
where our two names are inscribed, close to one another.

In inscrutable Greek calligraphy,
the Pythia described our passion,
our first kiss. She wrote words
that didn't say, didn't hide,
but signified.

There is also a manuscript written in old Carolingian,
gilded, illuminated in azurite
and vermilion, carrying the verses of a monk
who could see future lives.

Our names are joined together
in a paragraph dripping with destiny.
There is our love, our separation,
all your women, all my travels.

Summer House

We shell peas and grill fuzzy peaches.
Children run and play
in the commons, their voices
rising through the open windows.

Winds are a constant chatter, both from the Garda
and from Trieste. They sweep
through the house, agitating curtains
scattering thoughts.

I make lavender oil
and drizzle it in random corners.
I never think of you
any more.

At night, sometimes, I sleep.

Stay

Don't go, dream of a lush underbush
we could find happiness right there
like Angelica and her Saracen lover.
We could find a clearing in the forest
stay a while and listen to the bubbling brook.

Don't go. Stay with me for another
few minutes. It's a dark forest I know
and I can't make it any more luminous for you
but we can remember that one time
when you thought you loved me.

Please stay. The alarm clock is ringing
and you are fading away.
My dreams are wide open, come back.

One More Dream

August rains revive the forest
our dreams keep coming back.

It is finally raining
we pull out the light blanket
fragrant of citrus and sage.

And it's good that the thunderstorm
wakes me up and interrupts
the heated argument
I was having with this man
in my sleep
when I slapped him in the face
his beloved face I just wanted to kiss.

Robinson Avenue

In this spring of thunderous rains
of blessings all over god's country
there's a new for sale sign
near my house.

The neighbours had a baby, our homes
too small for a nursery
and a playroom.

They will move away from the river
in a little enclave full of children and moms
dads mowing lawns and trimming hedges
milk cartons in blue boxes on recycling days
delivery boys slinging rolled-up papers
on the sidewalk.

Mulini

Everyone loves
the old water mill in Portogruaro:
the turning of the wheels over the lazy Lemene
the ducks, the boisterous waterfall.

As a child my father took me to *Tre Scalini*
with him. He'd have white wine
and fried calamari hot from the kettle –
I would get one too.

Now *Tre Scalini* is a ritzy restaurant where I take
my guests – colleagues and visitors.

The CEOs inaled the lasagna with mussles
touching my arm, as though wanting to say
something, but exiting my life in a whisper
never mind the scattered corpses.
He preferred not to describe
the algohythm of distance
the algebra of never again
the most lacerating so long
soon to befall us the next morning.

Getting Ready

To watch him from the other room,
get up from the bed,
extract a perfectly ironed shirt
from his overnight bag
hear him whistle, shave
with the Mac3 razor
that would not blemish his delicate skin.

See him slip on knee-high socks,
and that Etro shirt,
making the usual joke about Etro's shirts,

and whistle, his mind already somewhere else
someone waiting for him by a lake
of which I was supposed to suspect
nothing at all.

Between Two Full Moons

It is the job of the moon to rise
high over Taormina close to midnight.

It is my job to not dial the number,
full moon over Taormina notwithstanding.
It was my only job
to not give in to the moon's undue influence.

I failed.

So I can't blame the full moon if I called
and he answered, if he spoke to me
with winged words, if my hopes realighted.

A month, a summer, a lifetime.

The moon's only job was to light up the sky.
Mine was not to surrender to dangerous dreams.
The moon accomplished the brightest light.

Of that Season

Of that season I remember
the agony of understanding.
Of that year I remember my broken
ligaments, and his broken promises.

Of that summer I remember calling him up
under the spell of a fool's moon over Taormina
and hearing his voice
his endearing, soothing voice
his whispers.

Mornings Are so Hopeful

I wake up and my father has a high fever.
He never admits to illness.
But I gather a thermometer,
Tylenol, water. I make a cup of tea.

He takes it all begrudgingly and stays
in bed, asks me to read the thermometer
or get his reading glasses in the kitchen.

Twice more he asks me to check his temperature
which keeps going down, 40 to 39 and then 38.
After three hours he gets up, like a boxer
hit on the ring on the ten-count.

He gathers his forces, coughs and declares
that he needs to tend to the chickens in the coop.
He shaves in slow motion,
gulps some espresso and says: "Look at me
all healed already."

Paros

I wake up in front of a chattering palm,
my forehead swept by night winds.

Swallows have taken residence
outside my window, and this house
is translucent of Parian marbles,
every hue of pure white.

At the beach, I collect marble stones
honed by the tide. On them I write
names of Greek deities and prayers
let the Aegean take them away.

Winds

The first sound out of my dreams
is from the swallows nested
on the exit light. The two chicks
left the nest yesterday
the parents are alone again.

Early in the morning
the town is an amphitheatre of white homes
that breathe in unison.
They take up a coral tinge
as the pink fingers of dawn
grab them and make them blush.

Caterina makes coffee in the great hall
and we all gather around like birds.
When the winds increase
the first window slams, then the second
and the third. The curtains billow.

Invisible fingers pick up the rhythm
the entrance glass doors slams against its frame
and we all run around to save
the window panes from shattering.
The bed sheets outside are teased
into performing a frienzied dance.

The women start feeling a tingle in their loins
bees in their skirts abuzz.
The guys look at them with renewed interest.

Hometown

Growing up, the park
was bristling with used syringes,
the walls of the medieval houses were
greying and peeling away.

We all suffered
from a sadness of the soul.
But I rode a Vespa 50 Special
which that gave me freedom
if not joy.

The countryside in the summer
was fragrant of cut dandelions,
marshes and mosquitoes.
We went by the railroad to pick
flowers from the acacia trees
fry them and eat them
with a dusting of sugar.

Then I left; my town changed,
money poured into it like a rainfall
now it is a jewel
with a tourist office and postcards.

And when the CEO visited,
amidst all the excitement and words
he said it is all so pretty here.
I can't imagine why you left.

Fields and River in Love

In love with these fields
that embrace the river,
that tickles the ducks,
that travel V-shaped over the reeds
moving slowly in the waters
that make love to the countryside.

Lazy river that slithers to the sea
silted in with reeds and ducks
nets and mysterious eels.

In the distance, the burgundy houses
make love to the cerulean sky
and all we know the woman who lives there
whose lover left her, who is seconds away
from calling it a day.

Trees

Wet hair, wrapped in a cocoon on top of my crown chakra.
I get dressed and stop by my laptop. No word from you.

Outside my window, the river is a chattering ribbon.
My fingers walk daily through your web site
perhaps you have, indeed, forgotten me.

My mind is bolts and thunders across that ocean,
to your outstretched arms, that I only fantasize about.

A golden light descends upon the city,
friendly are the maples trees
with their arms flailing in the autumn winds.
To be held by you, like these trees would.

Final Exams

Another semester is over,
and I am out of here. So many years of this,
I forget most of their faces
the tension and hope in their eyes
during finals.

Alex comes in late, hair sticking up
glasses askew, stumbling onto the backpacks
lined along the wall.
Sandra Takashi, from Rio de Janeiro,
writes her exam in golden ink, oblivious
to the office's photocopying obsession.
I tell myself the glittery ink is all for me,
a metaphor to a cheerful goodbye.

Ursula, my star student, brings me a cookie
before the exam
I saw her eyes brimming with tears
the second class of the semester
as desks in the classroom were too tight.
I am too large, she said, last year I was thinner,
it's all my fault. I try to console her
and we move to another classroom
where she spends the semester
squeezed inside slightly larger desks.

Diego, the Cuban doctor, also my student,
at the end of a hellish semester
runs into me in the hallway
and blurts out: "Ti amo."
His eyes sparkle mischievously, little wrinkles
fan around them. I tell him: "Lo so, lo so."

I'll Call

When I leave for this heart-wrenching journey, I'll miss our frozen land, its long sunsets. But I'll be sure to call you while I am gone.

I will be in a city with quiet rivers, the one of many revolutions. Amidst little cafés and *boulangeries*, I will call you, we'll have breakfast on the phone.

My brother will meet me in a small country full of freckled women; they speak three languages there; I will whisper to you in each one of them.

From the banks of the Congo, in the bosom of my broken-hearted family, I'll be thinking about you. I'll choose a white Panama to wear, I'll call you on the cell.

On the way back, I'll visit your brother's house by the almond-shaped lake. We'll talk about you and miss you. I hope you'll be home when we call.

I promise, I'll come back. You'll hear from me just as soon as I return.

Imelda

Ah well. There is sex, food and swimming
in a blue ocean. And then there are
shoes. So here I am, here's the Shoe Temple,
the Handbag Taj Mahal, the Suitcase Basilica.
And the *signorine*. Not just generic ones,
but *shoe signorine*, those who help you navigate
the endless isles, who know your heart by heart.

They can tell you want something *red*
from the way you walk in the door.
All you need to say is: comfortable,
and they'll answer softly: I'll get it for you.

Try this, try that. My own *signorina*
is tall and blonde, switches in and out of Italian,
two Northeast dialects – and German, for the sake
of a couple of Austrian tourists in need of a shoe fix.
All the while, she offers personal, suggestive
advice, such as: oh, your lover will just *adore* you in these.

She's gentle and blue-eyed. Kind of like the sister
I never had. She does not mention my chubby
feet, but uses exquisite euphemisms, such as:
soft. It would be lovely to have
her, instead of my ruthless superego.

My feet, they drift among clouds
of leather and foam, the sounds that carry over
conversations with other customers,
and a flutter of heels, the door that opens and
closes, the celebratory ring of the cashier.

And suddenly, I am lonely. Not sure why
I want so many shoes.
Perhaps it's the charm of these *signorine*
which is so hard to come by in real life.
Perhaps I just consume, therefore I exist,
counting on *Prada* for happiness,
Café Noir for nourishment.

I pay my 95 Euros for a pair of red boots.
The owner gives me a 2-Euro discount
("Have yourself an espresso," he suggests with a smile)
while my mind is already on that pair of sandals
I might purchase next week.

Last Sips

We took a few last sips
of the blond house wine
brought out by a waitress named
Amalia – what else –
while the other Amalia in the back
embroidered a tender *fado*,
complex and obscure like destiny.

The owner, smiling with a wide, uncorrected
diastema, served warm chocolate cake
with glasses of translucent Port
– aged ten years, aged twenty –
until we could take no more sweetness,
no more moonshine laced with honey.

We took the last gulps of Oporto air
flowing like a shy maiden's breath
as I longed to share some of it
with you, probably asleep,
back in Milan.

"You are the only thing
missing here tonight,"
I texted to your outpost in the Po valley
drowned in summer fog.

Gentle breezes lolled us to the bank
of the Douro as we took in the daring curves
of the Eiffel Bridge, the inadvertent
harmony of lights raising from the other side.

Those Gray Saturday Mornings

On Saturdays, we would dress up
and go out to buy bread. I was 5 years old.
I would walk behind my father in the old piazza
by the marble monument to the unknown soldier
and the Ghibelline townhall.
He would stop at the café by the river.
He'd tell me to be careful on the three marble steps
that divided people from water. I would
always look for trout, saw none.

The small chapel rising from the river
is consecrated to the Madonna of the Fishermen.
The smell of fried calamari ensnarled us.
For the men in the bar, fried fish
was the best excuse for wine.
I would get one calamari ring
(hot, fragrant, salty)
and drink orange soda.

Before going home we usually stopped at the newsstand
buy *Il gazzettino* and a comicbook for me.
There were no duties, no end in sight.
The best time was on those gray Saturday mornings,
when the men gathered at the café
and predicted more rain.

Virgins

Since they call it extra virgin, as if virgin
would not suffice, one thinks of olive oil
as something ethereal and pure.

But where the sun is hotter and the land drier,
olives are not hand-picked from branches,
but beaten off trees. They are thrown
in baskets, taken underground, to a *frantoio ipogeo*
where they are squashed, and swished around
until they release a drop or two.

They all come crashing down together,
ripe or not, intact or bird-eaten,
with twigs and leaves. From the beating
of the ancient branches comes an even thicker
communion, one that bridges
the chasm between the chosen ones
and the others.

Outer Layers

I won't tell you where, you said,
it's a surprise. A little alpine lake,
a gem in the hands of Oshun
goddess of fresh water and patience.

Digging through your outer layers
was strenuous work.
Your mind a metamorphic rock,
stratum upon stratum of glittery
formations, immeasurable like the universe
that might have thrown you my way.

Around the lake, a forest,
a green epiphany: emerald and jade,
moss and avocado, lake foam and fern.
I gave you a rose quartz to keep
for protection, I said, for love.

I'll do something, you promised,
as it was the day before
the day I left. Emotions running raw
as you whispered to the forest, or me.
I know nothing of you
I thought, bathing in your blue light.

Sant'Anna in Camprena

Not just another saint in the calendar,
not just the patron of childbirth
and sick babies, she's the Sant'Anna
presiding on fecundity and harvests,
adorned by a shadowy
Etruscan word, Camprena,
whose sound loomed mysteriously
as we walked uphill.

When the road became too narrow
the bus driver said he would wait for us
right there. We tiptoed on a white gravel path
through the sepulchral countryside.
Fig trees bathed in the orange light
of the incipient sunset,
accompanied by the sombre whispers
of cypresses and pines.

A monastery with narrow parting
windows, a tower, a Franciscan chapel,
and a dog, cats, chickens. Downhill,
the ancient land, manicured for millennia,
mostly sold to foreigners.

There were refreshments, of which
I remember the unsalted bread,
the goat cheese and the melon juice.
The abbey had rooms available for guests,
but we were there just to look at Sodoma's
paintings in the refectory.

His nativity, last supper, crucifixion,
were frayed like an old quilt. We marvelled
nonetheless at the grace of the draping
of a dress, at the elegance of the curve of a neck.

One of my colleagues, the architect, brochure
in hand and glasses down his nose, whispered:
don't tell your foreign friends about this place,
let's keep it all to ourselves.

Tornado

Driving to Angela's I stopped
at a Shell gas station. That's all the time
it took: coming out of the restroom
the sky had turned purple and the sirens
wailed like angry banshees.

Other people waited it out inside the gas station,
amidst jars of peanuts, corn chips,
cigarettes and break fluid.
Two guys by the counter spoke Swahili –
when the light went off I thought that, perhaps,
one of them might kiss me.

The sky and the ocean melted into cobalt blue
on the right, baby blue on the left.
I woke up before being kissed,
never got to see the tornado hit.

Two Books

I am a page of South American magical realism
perhaps not the kind that might win
the Nobel Prize, but a slower,
more derivative dribble, in which someone
cries while cooking a meal
and the whole family is taken by such great
forlornness that they weep in arousal
all over the second course.

You are poetry by Medbh McGuckian
vertiginous and obscure. I am children's
lullabies, stories of crocodiles in love
pellucid, a bit simple.

As your riddles stammer out of the page
I read them hoping to crack the code
but your words are opaque
a roaring river of dark dreams.

I am lost in the depth of your secrets.
But if you came back, and showed up
at my office with a smile as a gift,
I would attempt an understanding, I would.
I would try and get you, one more time.

Venice

Jasmine flowers exhale their drunken smell
under a bridge. The trunk of a stone
elephant sticks out of a souvenir store.
Venice is apricot and swordfish, the bronze man
shaping his soul against the mirror of the waves.

Apples and ginger at the open market
the feeling that it could have been
different, had you been here, with me.

Children still play ball in Campo Santa Margherita
the fountain one of the goal posts.
We drank from it once, you and I.

Up and down small bridges
I hold hands with someone new.
I try to lose myself in this love story,
in some other canal, in the eyes
of this city fragrant with cinnamon,
brimming with watermelon juice and tears.

I would have something to say,
not to him, but to you. Something precise,
such as, it's four-thirty and I miss you,
my renegade universe and inexisting
future – but you are nowhere to be found,
except for your effigy, that I see
in every stone of this city,
and for occasional emails, that rain into my iPhone,
and I read surreptitiously under the Rialto bridge.

Why Mailmen Carry a Belly Pouch

Because on the first sunny day in February
I walk the line between sickness and sunlight.
Somewhere on Main Street
I meet with a snowy friend of mine,
the female Samoyed who lives
with the hairdresser. On warm days
she lies like a pillow on the lawn, the tips
of her white coat shimmering like tinsel hair.

I wonder how it happened.
A hairdresser looking for living quarters
and salon space. Perhaps he walked down Main
on a bright day and saw a FOR SALE sign
on an ex-church. This looks good, he might have said.
Why don't I buy a Samoyed to go with it,
so I can brush her in my spare time.
The plaque at the corner says AD 1938.
The extant bulletin board might have once announced
PRAISE THE LORD! or SUNDAY SERVICE 10:30.
Now it says nothing. The church, transformed into a temple
to keratin, has Aveda stickers
on the stained glass windows.
Main Street is but a small detour on the way
to Janet's, whose chai is always ready,
hot and frothy and let's not try to find a simile for that.
Especially with this ailing heart after the fall
of my latest fruit of forbearance, my most recent
crux desperationis. Because the way I feel now,
there are too many hours in a day
before I can sleep again.

The pillow-dog bats her white eyelashes
and barks softly from the church parvis.
The corners of her mouth curl up in a canine smile.
Upon request, she might sit graciously,
even when one nests the word "sit" in a complete sentence:
"could you sit for me please." She might walk
around the yard to take a small bite
from a patch of virgin snow,
or hug your leg with careless abandon.

Two tiny terriers follow the mailman
across Main, and it is smiles and tail-wagging
all around. Man greets Samoyed,
who regally yawns in return.
With great ceremony he extracts
a cookie from his front purse,
while she performs a small dance
of anticipation. Her happiness
is so pure that the mailman smiles
and my soul
breathes
again.

With my Tongue

With my tongue I can catch you, flying off
the highest skyscraper of metonymies
falling though a sky of Edna St.Vincent Millay
poetry where all we talk about is
home-made marmalades and checkered
tablecloths. Where was I.

Oh, here: with my tongue I can catch you
flying.

I wash my hair with sparkling sunshine.
Not quite true, I wash my hair with a brew
of thorny flowers and porcupine quills
so I'll be prickly to the touch
when you come close to me. Which is,
never again.

I can forgive a balloon for being over
inflated, but can I forgive you for the same?
I could eat almost anything: blackberries right off
the bushes and even shadowy mushrooms
that grow very far from here. I can eat metaphors
with a spoon. And you.

Astral Selves

Outside the whirring sucking sacred cool penumbra
of San Pietro in Volta,
in one of the days when we still spoke
but were as furious with each other as ever
in one of those blessed and cursed days
you told me: not a day goes by
that I don't think of you.

Anytime I ride the train on the Bridge of Freedom and enter
Venice
it's a vacation with my past, and you.
But one day you grabbed me by the elbow
let's go you said, and as long as we were in the same
town, it was the immutable laws of gravitation
to rule, like over the sun and the moon.

And now, on a day in late May that smells like
winter in the Hebrides
after I received multiple degrees just to show you
now I feel that love is like a tattoo
of a naked ballerina on one's biceps
hard to get rid of, or to ignore
when one is alone. When your astral self
enters the window through infinite distances,
to remind me of the time we promised
never to be apart.

To Sleep on the Naked Earth

So many times this river has protected my dreams.
If you were here I would take you down to the old mill
in Boldara; they say a Dutch artist bought it,

restored it and displays geraniums on each windowsill.
Ducks and swans moved to this bend in the river;
do you remember when we fed them together?

It is cleaner now, and you can see the trout.
Can you hear this? Water rushing under the millstone,
thunder cracking in the distance. If you were here,

we would rush to the car, giddy with expectation
and lust. For lack of that, I bike to the river and lie
on the naked earth; being a fearless warrior

would be more fun if you could see me.
I would have liked to travel the world with you
the places we've seen together are precious few.

But a warrior cannot always choose the sky
that will cover her, or the company she keeps.

So I take you with me everywhere I go
on the hills of Ficulle, on the bend
of the Tajo in Toledo, up on the mesa in Acoma.

And here on the banks of the Lemene
where I rest. If I close
my eyes I can feel our lips touching.
Thank you for this kiss. And yes, it's me you sometimes see
with your mind's eye, even though I am on the wrong
side of the ocean, sleeping on the naked earth.

Go Lovely

Go lovely
peach, leave if you must.

The orchard will not remember you
the winds won't unfurl your fine fuzz
other fingers will split you open
another tongue will taste you
before summer is over.

Go sweet nectarine, leave if you must
the sun of my orchard won't warm your skin
the sweetness of the season
will soon abandon you
you will shrivel up faster
without my tender care.

But let us try not to let you
go, tender apricot, let us capture
the blush of your drupe
let's savour it, remember
it always, plant your seed
in the best spot in the orchard,
let's water it daily, tend to it amorously.
Help me watch it grow.

About the Author

Cristina Perissinotto is Associate Professor of Italian Studies at the University of Ottawa, where she also directs the Medieval Studies Program. *Tigers and the CEO* is her third poetry collection. A previous collection, *Exhale, Exhale*, was also published with Guernica.